George John Romanes

A Selection from Poems

George John Romanes

A Selection from Poems

ISBN/EAN: 9783744712170

Printed in Europe, USA, Canada, Australia, Japan

Cover: Foto ©Thomas Meinert / pixelio.de

More available books at **www.hansebooks.com**

TO

FRANCIS TURNER PALGRAVE

*in memory of his interest in the following poems
and of his affectionate regard and respect
for the writer*

INTRODUCTION

IT was among the wishes of my friend Mr. George John
Romanes that a selection from his poems should be
published, and Mrs. Romanes has asked me to help her
in making the selection and to write a few words by
way of introduction. Neither office is easy. The work
of many writers is an artistic creation which may be
understood and treated quite apart from the creator.
That is not the case with my friend's poems. He left
a considerable body of them. All had grown naturally
out of his everyday life, and are in a sense autobiogra-
phical. It follows that to illustrate his life almost every
poem is of equal importance, and also that the true key
to each and all of them is nothing less than the man
himself. The best introduction, then, will be found in
the 'Life and Letters'[1] which Mrs. Romanes has put together and given to the world. To that work this little
volume is a sort of note or supplement, the poems here
selected being intended to indicate rather than represent

---

[1] *Life and Letters of George John Romanes* (Longmans, Green & Co.,
London, 1896). The chief reference to the poems is contained in pp. 228
et seqq., where two very interesting and laudatory letters will be found, one
from Mr. Gladstone, and the other from the late Dean Church.

an aspect of the man without which his portrait and the record of his many-sided sympathies are incomplete, and to give in his own language some illustrations of the tenour and history of his interests and his thought.

George John Romanes was born on May 20, 1848. His father was a scholar and divine, being a Doctor of Divinity and professor of Greek at Kingston, in Canada. He may, then, have inherited a gift for language. He did not, however, himself receive any very strict education, and in particular seems to have had little or no definite grammatical or stylistic training. Nature as seen at home and in foreign travel, especially during a prolonged residence at Heidelberg, and later on in sport in Scotland, music and religion, these were the influences under which his early years were spent. At nineteen he passed to Cambridge. Here religion and natural science in turn dominated him and strove for the final mastery. His Burney Prize Essay on the subject of 'Christian Prayer and General Laws,' as has happened in the case of not a few students afterwards distinguished—a fact which is the best defence of these prizes—was at once the exercise and the proof of the main bent of his mind and genius.

He left Cambridge a thinker, a writer, and a natural investigator. Fortunate in the possession of independent means, he was able to pursue his researches and his meditations with the stimulus of the scientific circle of University College, London, and also in the solitude and seclusion of his own retreat and laboratory at Dunskaith, in Ross-shire. ' *Carmina secessum scribentis et otia quaerunt.*' It was here that the impulse and the inspiration to attempt verse-writing first came to him, the most felt and potent influence upon his whole nature at this time being undoubtedly the close friendship to which he was admitted by Mr. Charles Darwin.

His writing poetry seems to have begun about the time that he made Mr. Darwin's acquaintance. He published a few poems anonymously in magazines not long after this time, but the first to which he put his name, the most ambitious he ever wrote, was his Memorial Poem composed for the occasion of Mr. Darwin's death.

The second landmark or epoch in his verse-writing was, so Mrs. Romanes tells me, the death of another friend, in 1886.[1] After this he wrote much more frequently. In 1890 he moved from London to Oxford, and the remaining years of his life, except in so far as they were broken by travel in pursuit of health, were mainly spent there. In this his Oxford period his poetry seems to enter into a new phase both of feeling and form.

That a man of science should also be a poet is not, or at any rate ought not to be, extraordinary, any more than that a poet should be in some sense a man of science. For the two characters to be united in anything like perfection is, however, in modern times certainly

[1] Cf. *Life and Letters*, pp. 178, 179.

rare, although there is, as all know, the famous instance
of Goethe. The differentiation of function and special-
isation of effort increasingly necessary in the modern
world render this natural. In earlier times, when
natural knowledge, so far as it existed, was mainly a
matter of common general observation with the induc-
tions or intuitions to which it gave rise, natural
philosophy was closely allied to and often or usually
uttered itself in poetry. Notwithstanding their famous
feud with poetry, the early Greek philosophers were as
often as not poets themselves, while Lucretius, one of
the most poetical, is also the most truly scientific mind
of Rome, not a mere collector or cataloguer, like
Pliny, but a man of scientific observation, attitude,
and reasoning. Of so-called didactic poems, on scientific subjects, the ancient world of course offers many
examples, and in imitation of the ancient world our
own literature also, down to the end of the last century,
had plenty of them, among the last and not the least
being the once famous and famously parodied 'Loves
of the Plants' of Dr. Darwin. In this century such
compositions have fallen out of fashion. Natural science
has gone beyond them. The exact detail which it
requires is fatal to poetry. But it does not follow that
a poet may not have a scientific mind or a man of
science a poetic one, much less that the poet may not
also conduct investigations or the man of science write
poetry on the topics on which poetry is usually written.

Lord Tennyson has shown again and again, in

epithet and phrase as well as in longer passages, how the truths of observation, the great ideas and speculations the vistas and *aperçus* of natural science may lend themselves to poetry. Born in the same year with Darwin, he appreciated the great scientific movement of his time long before most men had grasped its significance ; he kept up with it and was interested in it to his latest day, and it was his well-grounded belief that in the still greater expansion and discovery which he foresaw, the poet of the future would have a yet ampler opportunity than had been the lot of the poet of the past.

On the other hand the late Professor Tyndall had distinctly something of the poet in his composition, and so had Professor Huxley. When Lord Tennyson died, among the many threnodies which appeared not the least striking was that of Professor Huxley, and among the most striking was that of the Duke of Argyll, who has since in his published volume more fully demonstrated that the scientific philosopher may also be to no small extent a poet. Darwin himself, although, as he has described in the passage only too well known in his autobiography, he allowed the sense to become atrophied, had in his youth a great fondness for and an excellent taste in poetry. In his ' Voyage of the " Beagle " ' he quotes his Virgil with a happy naturalness and appositeness which does credit to his love of good verses and to his Shrewsbury training. And if in old age he forgot the taste the effect was never lost. Darwin's style is not only always a distinguished literary style, but at times is

in the best sense highly poetical.   There is no passage
in the verse of his grandfather Erasmus so poetical as
the concluding page of the ' Origin of Species,' a passage
which reminds the classical scholar of nothing so much
as of Lucretius, even as 'Lucretius more than any other
ancient seems to anticipate in some of his observations
and generalisations Darwin himself.

The pieces here collected, however, are for the most
part not scientific poems, but the poems of a man of
science.   Few of them deal with scientific subjects at all ;
few even deal directly with nature, and those which do so
show not more but perhaps rather less minute observation than the poems of many professed poets, such as
Lord Tennyson, for instance, or Lord de Tabley or Mr.
Robert Bridges.   They deal with the themes natural
and proper to the poet and personal to the writer,
his loves—not his hates, for he had none, but his loves—
his hopes, his fears, his joys, his sorrows, his passion
intellectual and personal for Mr. Darwin, his love of
wife and child, sister, relative and friend, especially his
playful and graceful chivalry towards the young girls
of his acquaintance, his warm-hearted affection for
the lower animals, notable and welcome in one who
felt it so often his duty to use them for purposes of
experiment, his frankness and kindness to all and
sundry, his kindling sympathy with deeds of daring and
heroism, his interest in Nature and the country, in Art
and Music, and again his own inner and deeper thoughts

about the deepest of all themes, Life and Death, Man
and God. These are the topics of his verse, and running through them all appears the thread of his own
character, his largeness and loftiness of spirit, his love of
truth and of beauty through truth, his doubt yet his faith
in doubt, above all his hunger and thirst after righteous-
ness, a hunger and thirst most assuredly satisfied.

Such are the topics of his verse, and they are topics of
true poetry. Where Romanes was wanting, as he himself
was aware, was in art. An artist he does not claim to
be; a poet in the fullest sense he hardly claims to be,
for he came to be aware more and more, if he was not
so from the first, that although a great artist is not
necessarily a great poet a great poet must necessarily
be a great artist. If his verses are poetic in matter and
in spirit that is what the author claimed for them himself,
and that is all that he claimed. His own modest estimate
of them is set forth in the sonnet which he wrote
for his Preface, and it is just. He confined himself to a
few forms; his metres are not various; the rhythms are
somewhat monotonous and the diction plain. Rare
rhymes, novel turns, words curiously chosen there are
few, if any. It may be noted that he especially affected
the Sonnet, the defined scheme of which is a help to the
beginner and the amateur, but has often in the end
proved a snare and a trammel even to good writers.

His poems, then, have at once the merits and the
defects of amateur work. That they will fix the
attention or charm the ear of the world is not to be ex-

pected.   But they are part of the man, part of his voice,
part of his soul, the index and the utterance of a brave
and beautiful a loving and lovable spirit.   As such the
careful reader will, I think, as I have certainly done,
find them grow upon him in the reading.

They have, too, a pathetic interest.   They are the
utterance of a spirit which, as they themselves reveal to
us, was still in the making, still growing, still through
action thought and suffering, learning, struggling
toward the light, seeking after God.

One of the most powerful and touching of these poems
is the sonnet called ' A Hunt.'   As we read it we feel how
with sad prescience the writer anticipated what was
indeed the fact.   Disease crippled the singer and clogged
his song, and death all too early cut it short.   More it
seems probable he might have done in his art, as more
he would assuredly have done in thought, had he en-
joyed better health and a few more years of life, for
in both he was still beating his music out when his life
came to a close.

His latest poems as they are the deepest and ripest
in theme are also the richest and best in form and diction.
In particular the last written of all, the poem on p. 81
headed Hebrews ii. 10, is of all the most adequate in
expression, the most true to the best and deepest part
of his nature, the most arresting, the most worthy and
likely to live, the swan song of the writer's art, the
Nunc Dimittis of his faith.

T. H. W.

NOTE

The poem on Charles Darwin as here given is only a selection, amounting in all to about a quarter, of the poem as written and privately printed by Mr. Romanes. The other pieces are, with a few clerical corrections and verbal or metrical emendations, just as he himself left them, either in manuscript or privately printed. They are arranged partly according to subject, partly, and especially the later ones, chronologically.

CONTENTS

CHARLES DARWIN

A MEMORIAL POEM

B

I

THE hour of midnight struck upon the chime,
    And while with iron voice the mighty bell
  Roared from his open throat the doom of Time
    Each solemn clang upon my spirit fell
And held me listening in a solitary dread,
    While all the shadowed stillness of the night
  Stood tremblingly, as though some angel spoke,
    Stern, unrelenting, terrible in right,
Who gave the message in that steady stroke,
Then left the rolling sound through all the world
    to spread.

I heard it vibrate o'er the sleeping town,
    And wing its way with heavy beat afar ;
  It touched the River as he glided down
    The vale, and bridged his waters with a bar
Eternal, though the Night which crossed had left
    no trace :

The distant mountains caught the fleeting sound,
　　Re-echoed it to all the throbbing plain ;
And onwards still I heard it speed around
　　In widening circles, ne'er to meet again,
Dissolving in the moonlight through a world of
　　space.
　　　*　　　*　　　*　　　*　　　*

O Muse of Love, did Fame belong
　　To him I loved, and, loving, sing ?
If I should waft his name in song,
　　Would other voices tribute bring ?
Or would the name in silence fall,
　　As falls a snow-flake on the snow,
To mix and melt in one with all
　　Its fellows in the fleeting show ?
That name for me a charm would bear,
　　Should it be known to none beside,
Nor would it gain a sound more dear,
　　If Fame had spread it ocean-wide.

For he was one of that small band
　　Who in the waves of History
Stand up, as island cliffs that stand
　　Above the wide and level sea ;

And time will come when men shall gaze
   That ever-changing sea along,
To mark through dim and distant haze
   One rock that rises sheer and strong :
And they will say, ' Behold the place
   Where true was steered the course of
      Thought ;
For there it was the human race
   First found the bearings that they sought.'

But I must sing, my friend, to thee,
   As sobs the heart without a choice :
When thou hast been that friend to me,
   How can I still my weeping voice ?
Though all mankind in chorus sang
   The dirges of thy death, and earth
Through all her lands and oceans rang
   With praise of thy transcendent worth ;
And though mankind shall always sing
   The triumphs which to thee belong,
Though unborn generations bring
   New choirs to swell the mighty song,
     Yet I must add my single voice,
       Although I scarce may hear its sound,

At least by singing to rejoice
In hearing how my voice is drowned.

My help, my guide, my stay of heart and mind,
The friend whose life was dearer than my own,
Canst thou, whose kindness always was so kind,
Thus leave me now so utterly alone ?
Thou´canst not leave me in my sorest need,
Behold these hands outstretched in vain to
thee,
Oh, see the heart, which thou hast broken, bleed,
And tell me not that thou canst turn from me !
Say not, as others say, this grief is vain ;
In very madness truth may find a place ;
And I shall not believe, through any pain,
That pity can be frozen in thy face.
Though Death has fixed thy soul in wintry
clay,
Shall burning tears not melt the ice away ?

I see the pity melting in its eyes:
That face still watches me ; it still can bless ;
By day and night do I behold it rise,
And speak to me old words of tenderness.

If thou hast gone before, and I am left,
  Yet I can hear thee call where thou hast gone ;
And not for long am I of thee bereft,
  For, lo ! thy steps I follow one by one.
What time I cannot tread the lonely place
  Where I beheld thee pass beyond my view,
I yet can send my thoughts beyond my face,
  And almost meet thee there, where all is new :
    By thee, 'mid scenes before to me unknown,
    The beauty and the wonder to be shown.

Or can these thoughts of Hope before me flown
  Be but the shapes of madness in the air—
Thy voice a mocking echo of my own,
  And all the world a Castle of Despair ?
Am I the substance of a hideous dream
  (Whose unknown dreamer is a maniac mind,
Some God who made me not that which I seem,
  But forced me into being undefined),
A shapeless ghost created by His thought
  Who, in the ravings of eternal night,
Is thinking and unthinking systems fraught
  With horrors of His own distempered sight,

In gleams of such a mind a passing note,
Through universal madness left to float ?

Peace, desperate heart ; fight not against thy fate,
  Though newly stricken with the madding dart
And writhing in thy pain : 'twill not abate
  The wound to force its bleeding lips apart
With words delirious.   The struggle cease,
  And when the calm of Reason comes to thee,
Behold in quietness of sorrow peace.
  By such clear light e'en in thine anguish see
That Nature, like thyself, is rational ;
  And let that sight to thee such sweetness bring
As all that now is left of sweetness shall :
  So let thy voice in tune with Nature sing,
     And in the ravings of thy grief be not
     Upon her lighted face thyself a blot.

II

Old Abbey, beautiful and vast,
  Of this proud land the noblest pride,
Where history of ages past
  Is gathered in and glorified,

As tides which move with rhythmic sway
  In tall sea caverns come and go,
Beneath thy solemn arches gray,
  The generations ebb and flow.
Yea, thou hast seen a nation's life,
  With all its triumphs, hopes, and fears ;
The days of peace, the days of strife,
  And changes of the changing years.
Yet through all change one steadfast stream
  The stream of living hope and prayer,
The trust that all is not a dream,
  But that upon thine altar stair
There leads a way to God above,
  Within whose temple here they stand,
And who shall join, in endless love,
  The generations hand in hand.
And so the sacred dead are brought,
  To sleep beneath thy sacred floor ;
The mightiest men of deed and thought
  In generations gone before.

In fellowship of death they lie,
  Of all the sons of men most great,

A vast and peerless company,
    In motionless and silent state.
O ye who consecrate this place,
    Who forged the moulds of History
And cast the future of our race,
    How awful your solemnity!
Together, yet in death alone,
    All ye the noblest of your kind,
Whose every skull of crumbling bone
    Once held a world of living Mind.
Oh, where are now those worlds of Thought,
    Which rolled amid the skies of Time,
And seemed, with blazing lustre fraught,
    Of stars of glory most sublime;
Which held the life of Joy and Pain,
    And high Ambition's fitful glow,
And Love, which ne'er shall light again
    The zenith of a darkened brow?
        These empty spheres of ruin lie,
            Polluted, dark, and lifeless there;
        'But where those glorious worlds?' we
            cry,
            And all creation echoes, 'Where?'

The long procession waiting stands,
  Rank after rank, line after line ;
And far-famed men of distant lands
  All met in homage at his shrine.
The citizens, in pressing surge,
  Fill far the place from side to side,
While from the choir a sombre dirge
  Comes rolling through the arches wide ;
And then, when all is hushed and still,
  With motion slow the pall appears,
While tides of sorrow rise and fill
  The dried-up wells of bygone years.

For now of age the frozen eyes,
  Which long have coldly gazed on pain,
Once more are dim, and wintry skies
  Dissolve in drops of summer rain.
Forwards we move, with solemn tread,
  Through all the thousands gathered here,
Sing requiem music for the dead,
  Behold the sinking of the bier ;
While sorrow, swelling wave by wave,
  Seems on our breaking hearts to break,

And bury in that closing grave
    The hope which fainting wings forsake.
        My highest, noblest, best, O thou
        Unutterably loved and great!
    Farewell, farewell, for ever now—
        One word, one look—too late! too late!

Too late! too late!   For ever more too late!
    Oh, change all-overwhelming—absolute!
A change no thought can compass, gauge, or
        state!
    A change from highest being to a mute
And empty void!   The living man I knew—
    The mighty structure of a peerless mind—
The friend whose soul was open to my view—
    An ordered world, as definite in kind
As is this planet—full as are the skies
    Of systems within systems, reason-ranged—
All vanished—blotted out before mine eyes!
    This is the change; and with it I am changed
        To-day that universe for me doth end,
        Which lost a world who was my living
        friend.

Shall I not trust that mighty voice which cried,
    And shook me in my nature with its cry,
Announcing, when all other hope had died,
    The overwhelming truth, Thou shalt not die?
E'en from the grave arose the words it spoke,
    As though the heavy jaws of Death had moved
To belch them through the darkness that they
    broke.
    To Reason's eye those words may not be
      proved,
Which seemed but sounds to touch the list'ning
    heart;
    Yet why, among the senses of the soul,
Should I alone attend the seeing part,
    And not draw all my knowledge from the
      whole?
      I am a man, and but as man I know:
      Let Instinct speak where Reason fails to
      show.

I weep not for thy giant mind;
    Of thee that mind was but a part,
And if it had been uncombined
    With all the greatness of thy heart

The heavy edge of Sorrow's plough
　　Could not have trenched the heart it breaks ;
Nor would my grief have been, as now,
　　A grief my deepest soul that shakes.
Ye who thus speak but know the grief
　　Of those who grieve that genius dies—
A sorrow distant, small, and brief,
　　Which may not even dim the eyes.

But when the heart has lost those dear,
　　As father, brother, child, or bride,
It scarcely adds another tear
　　To think that with them genius died.
As rivers swallow up the rills,
　　Which find in them their natural goal,
One deep wide grief it is that fills
　　All channels of the troubled soul.
Although we know the dead were great,
　　And that afar their names were spread,
We care not then for Fame's estate ;
　　They were our own, and they are dead !

　　And thus it is for thee I weep,
　　　　Oh, more than with an orphan's moan :

Thy genius through the world may sweep ;
Thy love for me was mine alone.

I loved him with a strength of love
 Which man to man can only bear
When one in station far above
 The rest of men yet deigns to share
A friendship true with those far down
 The ranks : as though a mighty king,
Girt with his armies of renown,
 Should call within his narrow ring
Of counsellors and chosen friends
 Some youth who scarce can understand
How it began, or how it ends,
 That he should grasp the monarch's hand.

Love, thou art God ; and God is love :
 With man in man we find thee dwell ;
We know that thou art from above ;
 And call thy name Emmanuel.
Almighty Love, more strong art thou
 Than that which stands before my face !
Oh, quench the voice that asks me now,
 ' Why gaze ye into vacant space ? '

For thou to me art living breath ;
   I am in thee, and thou in me ;
Though all creation sink in death,
   Mine eyes should still be turned to thee.

So still we hope, and, hoping, say—
   Behold, we know not how or why,
But, feeling, know that, be what may,
   Love such as ours can never die :
Though Change shall move, and Time disperse
   These tabernacles of decay,
The Spirit of the Universe
   Is surely mightier than they.
Almighty Love, more strong thou art
   Than he whose hand is on my soul !
I hear thine answer in my heart,
   And cry, ' He cannot take the whole.'

More strong is Love than Death, we say :
   Then on the face of Death we see
An ashen smile that answers, ' Yea ?
   Ye knew his love : look now on me ! '
Almighty Death, we do thee wrong !
   Love made not thee ; thou madest Love :

And if thy creature seem so strong,
  It is thy strength that he doth prove.
From thee his living breath he drew,
  And in thy shadow gained his light ;
Thy being out of darkness threw
  This great reflection of thy might.

    And what thou gavest thou dost take :
      Thou canst not change before our cry—
      Not change, e'en for those dear ones' sake
      Who left us in our agony !

I am alone among the dead ;
  And this the place where he is laid—
One line of golden flame is shed
  By Hope, who, standing as a maid
In that high window, strikes the ray
  Of sunshine in her lamp down straight
Upon his marble tomb.   To-day
  'Tis Easter morn.   Can this be fate—
A dim, uncertain prophecy
  Which some far distant Easter Day
Shall in refulgence verify,
  When all that is has passed away ?

                                        C

The breath of Fame is like the wind
    Which blows the spray of autumn seas—
A voice that calls the ready mind
    To set its course before the breeze ;
And, not to let occasion fly,
    The listless joy of ease to scorn,
The bending oars of Thought to ply,
    While o'er the waves of Life is torn
The bark that rushes with the gale
    And heaves upon the foamy hills,
Exulting wide to spread the sail,
    Whose lap a growing tempest fills.

The breath of Fame is softly sweet,
    As summer wind on toil-dewed brow
When evening veils the noonday heat
    And shadow hangs from every bough.
'Tis then the man of mighty frame
    The sinews of his toil unbends,
Uprears his stature to the flame
    Of sunset's golden sky, which lends
Its light his gathered sheaves to show,
    All nodding in the harvest's breeze :

And then it is that zephyrs blow
    Beatitude on well-earned ease.

Fame is the joy in work begun—
    The knowledge of a strength declared ;
Fame is reward for labour done—
    Rest made delicious, strength repaired.
And if we work, as work we must,
    With hope that what we work is good,
No other measure can we trust,
    So purified from selfish mood,
To gauge the worth of what we do,
    Or show ourselves what strength we find,
As is the judgment, stern and true,
    Of many voices of our kind.

And if we bear our kind such love
    As noblest minds are wont to bear,
There is no joy to place above
    The consciousness that all declare
Our toil to be the toil of strength,
    Directed with a purpose wise,
And by our patience crowned at length
    With honour in a nation's eyes.

To be of man a mighty son,
　　Of Nature's womb a chosen child ;
The giant who delights to run
　　Mid shouts of welcome long and wild :

　　To feel that we have lived indeed,
　　　　And like a shelter raised our name—
　　This is to feel no other need :
　　　　It is enough ; and it is ·Fame !

For all that I have gained from thee, O thou
　　Who gavest me what only thou couldst give,
To thee my gratitude is rising now,
　　As from the Earth, ·in all her lands alive,
Goes up the morning incense to the sun.
　　Her deep, full heart of gladness in that cloud
Pours out the gratitude which every one
　　Of all her children breathes, or sings aloud :
The flowers opening gently their sweet eyes ;
　　The fields and forests shining in the dew ;
The rosy flush on the arousing skies ;
　　And life awakening to joy made new ;
　　　　All, all are breaking into thankful praise ;
　　　　And thus my thankfulness to thee I raise.

Not for the knowledge which thou gavest me,
  Though thou didst teach as few have ever
    taught ;
Not for the opening of mine eyes to see
  The wonders of a world which thou hast
    brought
Within the range of sight ; not for the change
  Which thou upon this earthly face hast wrought
By bringing Nature's truth within that range,
  And joining it for ever with our thought :
No, not for these this thankfulness to thee ;
  But for the grandeur of a monument
By Nature reared to our humanity—
  A wondrous vision, all too briefly lent,
    To show, in that great type of heart and
      mind,
    Her most sublime ideal of mankind.

Dear English home! to me how dear!
  What memories within thee dwell !
Can it be true that, standing here,
  I only see the outward shell
Of all that once belonged to thee ?
  Or can it be those memories

Alone shall come to welcome me,
  Once wont to meet with living eyes
And clasp of hands beyond that door ?
  Ye phantom inmates, watch these tears !
Do I not know each room and floor
  Where ye shall live through all my years ?

'Tis hard to think ye are but shades,
  When all the rest is solid stone—
That here there is nought else that fades,
  No other change, save this alone.
Yet sweet it is to think and see
  This home is spared by Change's hand,
With every garden, shrub, and tree
  Still standing as they used to stand.
Were it not so, and Change should steal
  Through this loved scene from end to end
When all had changed, should I not feel
  That I had lost another friend ?

The lilacs raise their tufts of blue,
  Laburnums pour their liquid gold,
The hyacinths of every hue
  Breathe fragrance forth a thousandfold :

A MEMORIAL POEM

In yonder ever-whispering shade
  The birds still twitter, flit, and sing ;
And can that mavis on the glade
  The one great change be pondering ?
It runs, and peeps, and listening stands,
  Then runs a space, and lists again :
No more, sweet bird, those bounteous hands
  On thee, or me, their gifts shall rain.

Again I walk in his own fields,
  And·in their blossom bathe my feet ;
I bless the fragrance that it yields,
  And feel the sweetness is more sweet
Than ever breathed from meadow floor ;
  For, like the charm of magic spell,
It opens wide a fastened door,
  Which closed on scenes I knew so well :
It seems I need but turn around
  To·see him somewhere far or near,
And that I soon shall hear the sound
  Of his bright voice break on mine ear.

The jangle of a world's discordant strife
  Hath slowly been resolved to harmony ;

A million voices jarred against thy life :
  Thy death hath tuned them into melody.
The nations join in requiem of praise—
  Thoughts, tongues, and creeds of every
      degree :
Within this temple hall we saw them raise
  That monument to Concord and to thee.
Majestic Marble, massive, cold, and pure !
  To mark the change a fitting form art thou—
A solid rock for ever to endure,
  And gaze on changing Time with changeless
      brow.
    For Truth is changeless as thy marble face ;
    And Truth it was that Change did here
        embrace.

Our wisdom is to trust them good ?
  A mocking laugh strikes through the air :
A smell of slaughter, warm in blood ;
  The shrieks of anguish and despair ;
The gasps of death, the cries of lust,
  With sounds of battle struggling fought !
Is this the darkness we can trust,
  And call it good ?   Away the thought !

To all the ravin and the wrong
   Shall we, who know the right, be blind,
Or say such things do not belong
   To those who think with human mind?

'Tis man, and only man can tell
   The evil from the good. Arise!
Behold! e'en though it be a hell
   On which shall gaze thine opened eyes!
'Tis we alone of things that live
   Such knowledge have attained; we know
That we alone can judgment give,
   Who bear the Truth upon our brow.
If Nature is a charnel den
   Of dead and dying, bruised and lame;
If Conscience only shines in men,
   Then let no man put out the flame.

   'Tis better, seeing wrong, to see,
      E'en though we cannot change the
        sight,
   Than saying, ' Things that are should be,'
      Or that ' whatever is, is right.'

From hunger, terror, pain, and strife
   The beauty of a world arose :
The life that grows to higher life,
   And ever lovelier as it grows.
The more the travail and the toil
   The more magnificent the birth,
Till, from the mound of senseless clay,
   We see the glory of the earth.
And what gave man the god-like thought,
   Or put that meaning in his eyes ?
What splendid truth has he been taught,
   Or with what wisdom is he wise ?

Then Evil is perchance the soil
   From which alone the Good can grow,
As knowledge only springs from toil,
   And toil makes precious what we know.
From Evil Good, and Joy from Pain,
   Derive their beauty and their light :
And knowledge of the Wrong is gain
   If it can teach us more of Right.
Or is there Right or is there Wrong
   Within the universal Whole ?

O God! an answer, deep and strong,
    Already sounds within the soul :
    ' Beware !   Who art thou ?   Stand and see !
Thy Conscience is for thee alone :
Raise not that voice in blasphemy :
Thou knowest not as thou art known.'

Let Faith and Reason here join hands
    As bride and bridegroom of the mind :
And only he who understands
    The world that union may unbind ;
For, lo ! the sons of Thought it gains
    In reason as in faith are strong ;
While universal order reigns
    No part can be which proves a wrong,
But highest reason, highest right,
    And greatest good must still ensure,
Even though with man should end the light
    Of all that men can deem most pure.
So let it be that, come what may,
    The very tomb which holds my dust
Shall bear the message, ' Though He slay
    Me, yet in Him shall be my trust.'

' Who art Thou, Lord ? '   We know Thee not ;
   We only know Thy work is vast,
And that amid Thy worlds our lot,
   Unknown to us, by Thee is cast.
We know Thee not ; yet trust that Thou
   Dost know the creature Thou hast made ;
And wrotest the truth upon his brow
   To tell Thy thoughts by worlds unsaid.
So help me, Lord, for I am weak,
   And know not how my way to grope,
So help me as I seek, I seek
   The source which sent that ray of hope.

   Teach me I have not understood :
      Thy ways are ways past finding out :
   Our wisdom still shall trust them good ;
      And in the darkness slay the doubt.

SONNETS

ETC.

PREFACE

BE it not mine to steal the cultured flower
   From any garden of the rich and great,
Nor seek with care, through many a weary hour,
   Some novel form of wonder to create.
Enough for me the leafy woods to rove,
   And gather simple cups of morning dew,
Or, in the fields and meadows that I love,
   Find beauty in their bells of every hue.
Thus round my cottage floats a fragrant air,
   And though the rustic plot be humbly laid,
Yet, like the lilies gladly growing there,
   I have not toiled, but take what God has made.
      My Lord Ambition passed, and smiled in
        scorn :
      I plucked a rose, and, lo! it had no thorn.

WHAT IS TRUTH?

I saw in dreams the Citadel of Truth—
  A palace as of polished silver, wrought
With precious stones.   Three god-like forms of
    youth
  Attempted entrance.   First a Giant sought
To force the door, besieging it with blows.
  He pausing, next a Child advanced with soft
Inquest ; and all about the pile he goes
  In ceaseless gaze, around, adown, aloft.
Last came a Greek-like maiden, fairy-bright,
  Who held in both her hands a golden key ;
The lock was turned ; in floods of rainbow light
  I saw her pass ; and then no more could see.
      .Where Thought and Science access failed
        to win,
        '.Twas Art that opened, Art that entered in.

ART AND NATURE

' I KNOW a bank whereon the wild thyme grows,'
    And there I lay me down to drink anew
The lyric dream of Midsummer. The woes
    Of Lear followed next ; and last I drew
Upon the ' sugared sonnets,' till methought
    Their sweetness with a lotus influence
Had bathed my being in a joy that sought
    To worship him who held its every sense.
Then on the page a creature from the grass
    Leaped forth—a living gem of Italy.
' Behold,' it seemed to say, ' how I surpass
    In wonder all the world of Poetry.'
        'Twas true.   Creative strength to God
            belongs,
        And weak its image in our greatest songs.

D

ON MY ARTISTIC BLEMISH

Is it that I love more than others love,
   Or that on me love doth the more bestow ?
   Or is it loving much that makes love grow ?
I wot not ; but I feel that far above
The grief which others tell doth my grief prove :
   For if the poets knew what I do know
   Of sorrow for the lost, they could not show
Such rays of joy as in their verses move.

They brightly sound the harp in major key ;
   The minor fills all truest songs I sing.
But how may Art supply the remedy,
   When through my thoughts a constant knell
      doth ring ?
O Grave, how absolute thy victory !
   O Death, how more than merciless thy sting !

CRITICISM

'Tis well to urge that Song should tell of things
  As various as Nature spreads to view ;
Verse sweeps her harmony from all the strings
  Of Life and Passion, not from but a few.
Thou speakest as an artist : I am none,
  ·Nor care to learn the wisdom of thy craft :
What melody is mine is mine alone,
  And seeks not any other strain to waft.
The bird of night, who sits in sombre grove,
  And sings of sorrow, sorrow, mournfully ;
The bird of day, who bursting full of love,
  Springs bathed in sunshine, sunshine, to the
    sky—
    These are the voices of an unlearnt art,
    And they the voices echoing my heart.

THE MUSE

I HEARD a poet to the gods complain,
  ' My muse is all so fitful, coy a maid
  That when my court most earnestly is paid
She smileth at my ecstasies of pain,
And shows her virgin shield of proud disdain :
  Yet, when abandoned, gentle and afraid
  Her voice will follow me o'er hill and glade,
To light anew a fever in my brain.'

I heard the answer speak in poetry :
  ' O highly-favoured child of mortal clay,
  Thou dost deserve that I, Apollo, slay
Thee in thy blasphemous impiety !
  Go, learn of her, who deigns with thee to
     play,
  The discipline of thine own constancy.'

SCIENTIFIC RESEARCH

Why should I chafe and fret myself to find
    Some pebble still untouched upon the beach,
    Where struggling wavelets follow each on each
Upon the tide-mark of advancing Mind ?
If, one with them and urged by those behind,
    My utmost energy at last should reach
    A stone unwetted by a bubble's breach,
What gain were it to me or to my kind ?

Though I should fail that further inch to go,
    Some other soon will creep its rugged floor,
While, resting on the conquered strand below,
    I calmly watch the rivalry before,
Rejoicing at the steady onward flow,
    But at my new-found peace rejoicing more.

LOVE AND NATURE

To lie beneath the summer of the trees,
　　What time they lift their lusty arms on high,
　　And flicker with their leaves against the sky,
In playful wrestlings with the wanton breeze ;
To watch the shadows stealing by degrees
　　Upon the river, lisping languidly
　　His luscious kisses as he passes by,
Amid the meadow murmuring of bees—

This is the joy that comes from absent pain :
　　But when, dear heart, thou sharest it with me,
All nature wakens to a new refrain,
　　And sings with gladness of a bird set free :
Though all else perish, and this still remain,
　　The world were Paradise, containing thee.

A HUNT

I saw a monster hunting with two hounds,
  Which snuffled on the track of unseen game ;
For far away, beyond the utmost bounds
  Of vision, lay the pasture of the same.
All day they tracked him, until he could see
  Them gliding through the valley like a spot ;
But basking in the noontide sun lay he :
  They were so distant that he heeded not.
So when at evening they surprised his lair,
  And dog by dog were hanging flank by flank,
He ran, and ran, and ran in his despair,
  Until, in midnight darkness, lo ! he sank.
      I ask the hunter of their names : he saith,
      We are Decrepitude, Disease, and Death.

GLORIA MUNDI

THE flower fades while yet the grass is green ;
    The trees are standing with their blossom
        shed ;
    The child I loved hath drooped her lovely
        head,
While reptiles crawl which Milton may have
        seen :
The higher life, that everywhere hath been,
    To lower life returns ere it be dead ;
    And, when all remnant of the life hath fled,
Eternal matter reigns as Nature's queen.

    Man is the blossom of the Tree of Life,
And mind the subtlest fragrance he doth bear ;
        So all that I have known, and thought, and
        felt,
    Of love, and hope, and fear, and peace, and
        strife,
        Before my very eyes ere long shall melt,
As melts a morning mist into the air.

THE DRAMA OF LIFE

THE flies are idling all and every day,
  The birds are shaded in the summer trees,
  While to the murmur of half-slumbering seas
The flocks and herds are dozing round the bay :
All Nature teaches me to pass away
  My little span of life in listless ease :
  What am I better than the rest of these
Her creatures, that I do not live as they ?

The mind that more than feels and sees and
    hears
  Is surely but as Nature's monster-birth :
To know the end before the end appears,
  Yet strive for things of everlasting worth—
This makes a comedy of toiling years,
  And man the dwarf who rouses gods to mirth.

DAY-DREAMING

Upon a day, in spring-time of the year,
  I sat a-dreaming where a willow stood,
  And watched my children playing in the wood.
Their joyous faces, and their laughter clear,
Aroused in me the once familiar cheer
  When I, too, was a child; till in the mood
  Thus caught, I murmured, 'Nature, thou art
    good!
'My little ones, my little ones, how dear!'

'Twas then I heard the voice of Nature say,
  Behold, thy children shall lie down with thee
In homes of death and heritage of clay.
  Yet, what was said but made them more to me;
And when they called that I should join their
    play,
  I went with them, ah! more than willingly.

MAN

THE world, indeed, is all a passing show ;
   But whence its origin ? and what its end ?
If I, amid its multifarious flow,
   Could find a purpose with its action blend,
In such a knowledge I could dare to know
   The pathos of the part that Man doth lend,
Be he the dwarf, whom heartless gods have made,
   To strut, deformed, the stage of comedy,
With hopes imparted but to be betrayed ;
   Or as a Titan, struggling with the sky,
And headlong hurled by that avenging blade
   Which yet again he rears him to defy—
      A giant or a pygmy, he is great
      Who bears the sorrow of a man's estate.

THE HEART

The chambers of the heart were made to hold
 Faith, Hope, and Love to God and Man ; these
  four
Give life and warmth where else were cheerless
 cold :
 If Doubt, Despair, or Hate break through the
  door,
To pillage, ravish, murder, and destroy,
 They leave a ruin to record their crime,
And Desolation fills the house of Joy.
 The tenement, enduring for a time,
Gives shelter now to evil birds of night,
 And beasts of prey ; while year by year it falls,
Decaying into dust. When these foes smite,
 And Sin alone is left to fill those halls,
  There stands, without a purpose, plan, or
   part,
  The crumbling form of what was once a
   Heart.

NATURAL THEOLOGY

ARRAYED in beauty did the world arise ;
  Arrayed in beauty doth it ever stand.
O children of mankind, lift up your eyes !
  Behold Him in the clouds, the sea, the land !
The firmament His glory doth declare.
  The hosts of Heaven, created by His breath,
As shining witnesses are standing there.
  O all ye skies, and all that is beneath,
Bless ye and magnify with endless praise !
  In us alone a stolid silence lurks :
The whole Creation else its voice doth raise.
  O Lord, how wonderful are these Thy works !
    Surely in wisdom hast Thou made them
      all !
    On Thee, on Thee let now Thy servant
      call !

Arrayed in order did the world arise ;
  Arrayed in order doth it ever stand :

But who declares the order to be wise,
　Or fondly finds in it a Father's hand ?
Oh, blind to what ye see, and deaf to all
　Ye hear ! The beauty is in your own eyes :
The loving words, which on your hearing fall,
　Are sounds which in your own poor hearts
　　arise.
What man among you, had he made this earth,
　But all his brothers would condemn to die ?
The parentage of such a monstrous birth
　Would brand him with inhuman devilry.
　　　Believe in love for man alone designed,
　　　Or else believe in God without a mind.

My soul was troubled by the sin and pain :
　My heart was withered by the thought of
　　God :
The order seemed an order to ordain
　Infinite Evil, with bad tidings shod.
This was the only minister of things ;
　And if I saw a beauty or a joy,
It was the beauty of a dragon's wings
　And folly of an infant with its toy.

Then, unawares, into mine idle hand
  A touch of sweetest childhood gently crept ;
A face was there that seemed my thoughts to
    brand ;
  A voice said, ' Father, Father,' and I wept.
      The trust which to a little child is given,
      Forbid it not a love that is of heaven.

MAN AND NATURE

Time was when Nature seemed more great than
　　Man :
　　To her Infinity ; to him the sky
　　Averted from a hunger-sunken eye.
But thou hast taught me, as no other can,
Within the compass of this little span,
　　A greater truth than her immensity ;
　　And now I see in what is born to die
The nobler purpose of Almighty plan.

O thou who thus unconsciously dost show
　　The one perfection I have found, to thee
I yield the highest reverence I owe ;
　　And Gratitude the whole wide world must flee,
Ere from this living heart it cease to flow,
　　Or bless the all that thou hast been to me.

HEREAFTER

WHEN I look back upon my childish years,
   And think how little then I thought at all,
Sometimes to me it now almost appears,
    So great the change has been, 'twere but a
       small
Increase of change that might transform a man
   Into a spirit, standing at the throne
Of God, to see in full the mighty plan
   Divine, and know as also he is known.
For why should thus so vast a growth have been,
   Which all but tops the verge of earthly skies,
If, at the end, all that a man hath seen
   Be blotted out before his closing eyes?
      So were it better still a child to be,
      And shout young laughter through a world
        of glee.

E

HEART AND MIND

IF all the dead whom I have known alive
　　Could rise unsheeted from their every grave,
What is the question I would first contrive,
　　And which the friend whose answer I would
　　　　crave ?
Not to the great philosopher or sage
　　My unreluctant tongue shall be untied,
Though in that hour I might believe an age
　　Of longing wonder could be satisfied ;
Not to the teacher of the ways divine,
　　Nor preacher of the faith he held on earth :
These well might follow in an ordered line,
　　As one by one the mind should give them
　　　　birth :
　　　　But, searching for one face, the heart would
　　　　　call,
　　　　Dost thou remember me, my all in all?

EX NIHILO

In all the universe that reacheth round
　The sense-imprisoned ken of man, no change
Can ever add unto the full abound
　Of that which fills the never-ending range
Of Being : combinations that arise,
　In ever-growing beauty as they pass,
And seem like new creations in our eyes,
　Are but as images in such a glass
As that with which our children cheat their
　　sight :
　Revolving ages ply the atoms' dance,
And when the game shall end, with fading light
　Shall end the many patterns thrown by chance.
　　　Or say we, Nature's fiery swaddling-
　　　　cloud
　　　Returns unchanged to constitute her
　　　　shroud.

Yet, lo! most wonderful of things on earth
    Is that which lieth nearest to our ken—
Conception of a thought which comes to birth,
    And springs to action in the world of men.
It comes to man amid that vast abyss
    Where his own nature reaches forth to blend
With all the universe that was and is,
    Without beginning and without an end.
It comes to him because he *makes* it come :
    He calleth it, and saith 'Appear! appear!'
And yet divineth not from what far home,
    Obedient, it riseth now and here.
        Yea, had it home in other mind or place,
        E'er thus it gazed, created, face to face?

BEETHOVEN

BEETHOVEN, let thy spirit call to mine
    From regions that no other eye hath seen,
    Or heart of man conceived. Stand thou
        between
The zenith of our thought and that divine
Effulgence of the Lord, whose fringes shine
    Upon the stars, in mercy spread to screen ;
    And when earthwards thy spirit still doth
        lean,
It is to fill our world with sound of thine.

Oh, great among the greatest of our kind,
    We hear its meaning where thy trumpets
        blow :
Beyond horizons thou hast left behind,
    And all the glory that the skies can show,
What thou hast found there is for us to find,
    As thou hast known it is for us to know.

AN INCIDENT OF STUDY

I READ and thought, and thought and read again :
The unrolled knowledge of the centuries
Made discord in mine ears, and to mine eyes
Displayed the tiny gleam which human brain
Had sought to cast, and sought to cast in vain.
 Ah, where was Truth amid these Hows and
  Whys ?
 What but a phantom mocking at the wise,
Whose wisdom ended in their fruitless pain ?

Then, in a moment, what a change was there !
A mighty language filled the very air,
 And Truth revealed with all the world was
  woven :
 My spirit sank, with shafts ˋof gladness
  cloven ;
For God Himself had witnessed my despair,
 And sent His blessed angel in Beethoven.

TWO PORTRAITS

Two portraits of the sweetest girl I know
   Hang side by side, and shed a ceaseless rain
   Of beauty, dazzling me with joy and pain :
For while the one will never deign to throw
A glance that even friendship might bestow,
   The other constantly sends back again
   The look that tells when hearts are knit in
     twain,
And follows me wherever I may go.

Ah ! why, if shadows thus their souls reveal,
   May not the substance with their motions
     move ?
Are masks to speak, and faces to conceal
   What all the passion of my soul would prove ?
Oh, Mary, Mary, for one moment steal
   The magic of those moving eyes of love.

TO EDITH

To other friends in sonnets I may sing ;
   How shall I sing, my greatest friend, to
     thee ?
   There is no song in any poetry
Which would not seem an all unworthy thing
If made to tell thy praise ; no voice or string
   Which man could tune may sound the
     minstrelsy
   That should be thine.   So let me silently
Place on thy tomb the blossoms that I bring.

As fullest feeling is by gesture shown,
   May these few lines but as a gesture seem ;
As deepest grief is heard in wordless moan,
   But as a sob do thou this sonnet deem.
No more.   The greatest friend that I have
     known
   Has vanished, like the glory of a dream.

FRATER LOQUITUR

O THOU who since my childhood's day was young
  Hast shared with me my every joy and pain,
  Who of the stars that come or stars that wane
Art still the holiest that has been hung
In all the skies of memory—among
  The lesser lights which move my idle strain,
  Why have I left the greater to remain,
As I have left thee, sister, still unsung?

Sole-balanced in the firmament on high,
  Two only orbs the form of kindred wear,
  And each to each in silent thought declare;
So we, like them, have filled each other's sky,
As joined, like them, in Nature's infancy,
  And each to each our silent witness bear.

PATER LOQUITUR

Of all the little ones whom I have known
　　Ye are so much the fairest in my view—
　　So much the sweetest and the dearest few—
That not because ye are my very own
Do I behold a wonder that is shown
　　Of loveliness diversified in you :
　　It is because each nature as it grew
Surpassed a world of joy already grown.

If months bestow such purpose on the years,
　　May not the years work out a greater plan ?
Vast are the heights which form this ' vale of
　　tears,'
　　And though what lies beyond we may not
　　　scan,
Thence came my little flock—strayed from their
　　spheres,
　　As lambs of God turned children unto man.

LIBER LOQUITUR

Take me from one who loves thee with a love
  More full than any of my language bears ;
In all my numbers see the spirit move
  Which thou hast shed upon my growing years.
Take me from one who in that spirit shares
  The greatest gladness that a man may find—
To entertain an angel unawares,
  Love-drawn from Heaven in form of human
    kind.
Take me from one who gives his all to thee,
  And of that all hath written here a part :
Yea, though the volume which thou hast in me
  Revealeth not the volume of his heart,
    Take me in token of a truth well tried—
    ' How much the wife is dearer than the
      bride.'

TO MY SETTERS

Most faithful children of your faithful clan,
    Embodiments of energy and grace,
    With eyes that glow in love, and on each
        face
Intelligence that might become a man !
No clockwork ever made more truly ran
    Than you in your co-ordinated chase—
    Now fast and free, then statued to your place,
A beauty group of black and white and tan.

Yes, fondle me to all your hearts' content,
    You dear old Countess, Bango, Sam, and
        Jill :
Ah, happy days those days together spent
    Amid the breeze of Achalibster Hill,
With miles of heather bathing us in scent,
    And bags as full as we could care to fill.

TO COUNTESS: AN EPITAPH

No more shall field and meadow, moor and
    grove
  Bid welcome to thy tireless energy ;
  No more thy master watch thy lifeful glee,
Who gavest all through all thy days to prove
One only joy all other joy above ;
  Whilst I, who stood instead of God to thee,
  Cared not thou couldst not share in thought
    with me,
When thou didst share that greater life of love.

For this it was thine only joy that lent,
  Which unto me my chiefest joy doth lend ;
And while in it thy creaturehood was spent,
  Where seek I else my creaturehood to spend ?
Then carve ye thus upon her monument :
  In death my fellow, as in life my friend.

THE SLOTH

Thou most absurd of all absurdities,
   Thou living irony of Nature's law,
   No wonder that in thee old Cuvier saw
Grim signs of humour in an otherwise
Not over-witty god : with ears and eyes
   Inverted, and each serviceable paw
   Transformed into a wretched hanging claw,
Thou hast turned topsy-turvy earth and skies.

' O " paragon of animals," why jeer
   At one who gazes with inverted eye ?
The " change of attitude " thou findest here
   Is my attempt to follow thine, and try
What benefit arises in this sphere
   By twisting all one's being towards the sky.'

TO THE ANTS OF TEXAS

Y E busy, busy people of the wood,
  When I behold you working every day,
  And marvel at the wisdom you display,
It seemeth but a questionable good,
That such high instincts as you show us should
  Be given you by Nature to obey,
  When all they serve, by all their wondrous
      play,
Is to conserve the life of emmethood.

But if such end such means can justify,
  Let other insects learn what this would show :
Our boasted thought can cast no sovereign eye
  Beyond the needs of life it needs must know ;
While, like this nest of ants, Humanity
  Doth ever sow to reap, and reap to sow.

TO A BUTTERFLY

THE battling labours of a Hercules
  Are in the hours of thy perpetual dance,
  Poor flutterer from the flowery meads of
    France.
Oh, cruelly ill-timed this southern breeze,
That bears thee now across the glittering seas,
  And mocks thee with an ever-lessening chance
  Of meeting with the far deliverance
Of England's happy whispering of trees.

Yet half the space thou dost already span :
  Such miles and miles those tiny wings have
    braved,
Thy world is changed since first their flight
    began ;
And if it seem, as far as eye may scan,
  A world where fields to ocean are enslaved,
  Endure unto the end, and be thou saved.

ADVERSITY'S CONSOLATION

A SPARROW saw a stricken Eagle's pain,
  As he fell headlong from the clouds on high,
  And chirped, with pity in her sideward eye,
' O monarch of the world, thy proud disdain
Of such a life as mine, when thou didst reign,
  Hath wrought this greater anguish here to die.
  Ah ! wherefore wouldst thou climb into the sky,
And scorn our happy flittings of the plain ?'

The Eagle answered, ' Anguish well may be
  When Heaven doth hurl a thunder from its
      wall ;
Yet anguish such as this destroys for me
  The terror that death brings to such as crawl :
  These mighty wings, that dared the deepest
      fall,
Await their end in peace unknown to thee.'

CHRIST CHURCH, OXFORD

CATHEDRAL in the silence of the night,
   Who lookest Godwards to the starry sky,
   Not proudly standing dost thou magnify
Thyself in distant earth-disdaining height,
Nor boast thy bulk a monument of might;
   But, worshipping in low humility,
   With folded hands and deep imploring eye,
Thou kneelest, as before the Master's sight.

The meek and lowly He exalts; so thou
   Hast gained a glory other shrines have
      missed.
Though least among them all, it is thy brow
   That wears the crown of the evangelist.
To thee let all thy princely sisters bow,
   O nursing mother of the Church of Christ.

FAITH

CAN it be true, as all the Churches teach,
  Nought is of Faith but what they hold as true?
Or is the Word set forth in human speech
  More sure than when revealed to human view?
Nay, if the truth be all that they would show,
  Let him who doubted be my witness here:
Faith's deepest joy were it at last to know
  That, while I knew it not, the Lord was near.
So now, with groping hands, I feel for Thee,
  Who hast such words as no man ever had:
Oh, count it sorrow that I cannot see,
  And not a sin that I was born so sad.
      Though dark the eyes that stream in sight-
        less grief,
      Lord, I believe; help Thou mine unbelief.

LOVE

When others sing the praise of those they love,
  I hear a voice that answers to mine own,
  As when the loud and deep melodious tone
Of some great bell wakes far a sleeping grove;
The faint responsive note doth sweetly prove
  How truly has another spirit known
  The meaning of the message that is thrown,
When all the powers of my nature move.

And why?   Because no other voice can tell
  The measure of the love that I have found;
Speak they however wisely, true, and well,
  They may not render back the full abound,
Where heart to song is as the swinging bell
  To distant echoes of a mighty sound.

II.

Yet I have seen the long-drawn billows roll
  Upon the concave of a greeting shore,
  And, as they broke along the sandy floor,
Lift up the voices of their ocean soul :
Then, like an angels' orchestra, the whole
  Great bosom of the land sent back the roar ;
  Deep called to deep, and, lo! the mountains
     bore
As vast a language as the watery goal.

In that one place I heard an echo wake
  To answer worthily a mighty tone ;
And I have found but one dear heart to make
  As infinite a meaning as my own :
There all that Love can give can Love retake ;
  Deep calls to deep, and deep to deep alone.

RELIGIONS OF MANKIND

HAVE I not seen ten thousand temples rise,
  In dome and pillar, minaret and spire?
Do I not know that Hope, with myriad eyes,
  From every zone doth gaze with one desire?
And back and back, since man on earth appeared,
  Has not the earth with such new radiance
    shined,
Henceforth a world by glittering hosts ensphered,
  That reach the answering looks of mind to
    mind?
Ah! can it be that all do vainly reach,
  By never-ending failure undeterred,
When, as the stars of Heaven, there is no speech
  Or language where their voices are not heard?
    Nay, rather let me join with all my kind,
    As one who knows of light though he be
      blind.

TARASP, 1891

TARASP, I leave thee with that fond regret
   Of one who dreams a dream of Paradise,
   And wakes to earth again with tearful eyes ;
For of all wonders mine have ever met
'Tis those—of forest, stream, and meadow—set
   Among thy giant crags, which pierce the skies
   Of sapphire with their snow—supremely rise,
And leave me now to die ere I forget.

So stand a Citadel of Memory—
   The time and place of this unearthly scene
   An ever-biding refuge of the mind :
So be that vision of sublimity,
   Which, having been, nought else can ever
      blind,
   O matchless valley of the Engadine.

MALVERN, 1892

To doze upon a sunny hill in June,
   And hear the lullaby that Nature lends ;
   To drink the cup that sweet contentment
     blends
With sweeter love of those whose hearts shall
     soon
Reverberate with joy, as they attune
   Their praise to praises that achievement
     sends—
   This is to feel that bounteous Nature bends
A mother's smile on manhood in its noon.

But when the shadows of the twilight come,
   And high Ambition needs must fold his wings,
While voices both of hearts and hills grow dumb,
   Can she still bring. the smile that now she
     brings ?
   Yea, by the memory of brighter things,
I'll trust her in the night that calls me home.

PSALM XXV. 15

I ASK not for Thy love, O Lord : the days
  Can never come when anguish shall atone.
  Enough for me were but thy pity shown
To me as to the stricken sheep that strays,
With ceaseless cry for unforgotten ways—
  Oh, lead me back to pastures I have known,
  Or find me in the wilderness alone,
And slay me, as the hand of mercy slays.

I ask not for Thy love, nor e'en so much
  As for a hope on Thy dear breast to lie ;
But be Thou still my Shepherd—still with such
  Compassion as may melt to such a cry ;
That so I hear Thy feet, and feel Thy touch,
  And dimly see Thy face ere yet I die.

FEBRUARY 11, 1892

IF God us twain should separate,
  When Death shall close our eyes,
Out of the deeps of deathless hate
  One deathless love will rise ;

And, stronger than the bars of Fate,
  'Twill pierce the nether skies,
To wing its way where one doth wait
  With deathless memories.

Then on and on, or soon or late
  'Twill reach those angel sighs,
And kiss at last, through Heaven's gate,
  With thine in Paradise.

EASTER DAY, 1892

THE house of mourning that I enter now
   Will never more rejoice in those glad eyes
Which looked upon their sorrow but to glow
   With deeper gladness in their purities.
For felt they not—yea, surely well they felt—
   Such loss was righted by a greater gain,
When all their blue blue innocence did melt
   Before our answers to their lightest pain ?
And knew they not—yea, surely they did know—
   That as our human hearts most utterly
From deepest fonts of love do overflow
     When all their gates are loosed by sympathy,
       So doth the very Fatherhood of Love
       In vast compassion most divinely move ?

Those eyes, alas ! we may no longer see ;
   But was not I that best and truest friend,
Who saw them from their very infancy,
   And saw them beautiful unto the end ?
And were they not so always wont to shine, .
   With fuller sweetness in their youthful light,

When, turning all the soul of them on mine,
  They shed affection as affection's right?
So I have claimed to harp the requiem lay;
  `Yet sound it not in any mournful wise;
For who would ask, upon this Easter Day,
  To draw her spirit down from Easter skies?
    Nay, let me sing as she would have me sing,
    Whose golden harp is loud with thanksgiving.`

Ah! let us join, my oldest friends and true,
  To greet with her this dawn of Eastertide:
It is the first that she doth drink anew
  The vine of Christ, and drinks it as a bride.
Then not for her, but for ourselves we weep;
  And if the days be not as they have been,
The time is short that we shall have to keep
  The flowers growing, and the churchyard green.
But now with her in choirs alternate ranged
  We sing an anthem angels have not known,
The psalm of man, by earth and heaven exchanged
    In mighty hosts and swaying antiphon—
      'Our house is left unto us desolate:'
      'Thy loving chastisement hath made me great.'

'HOW MUCH THE WIFE IS DEARER THAN THE BRIDE'

WHAT is there dearer than the maid is dear,
   Whose virgin love, aurora-like, doth bless
   Our whole wide world with golden happi-
      ness?
It is that maiden of another year,
When as our very bride she doth appear,
   Surrendering the charms we now possess,
   Which, sweet to watch, are sweeter to caress,
And grow more subtle as they draw more near.

But dearer yet, and much more dear than they,
   Is that sweet face the years now consecrate ;
Whose golden youth has burned itself away
   To silvery ashes of its first estate,
Leaving a love flame purified of clay,
   And great—aye, as the love of God is great.

TO ETHEL

ETHEL, thy name is as my breath to me,
    When on the breezy sunshine of a moor
    I draw the fragrance of the flowery floor,
Or walk along the foaming of the sea,
Where shores are lonely and the waves are free :
    It is the word to move a magic door,
    Where I, the fabled wanderer, lean and poor,
Become more rich than kings in finding thee.

Ah, sweet my treasure, what have I to give
    For more than all the wealth of all the earth ?
    Oh, take my heart and mind and life and
      soul—
    Take all I have—take all I am ; the whole
Is worthless, worthless unto such a worth,
Though I should have ten thousand years to live.

MADEIRA

Fixed on thy sapphire throne of sea and sky,
   And clothed with light as with a robe of gold,
   I see thee, in thy queenly state, uphold
An ocean sceptre o'er the mists on high,
Which wreathe thy head with crown of majesty.
   Yet in thy rocky arms thou dost enfold
   That child who came, when ages had unrolled,
To make thee smile upon his infancy.

What though it was some other womb that bore
   The tiny form thus wafted on thy wave?
Did he not bring a joy upon thy shore
   Which all thy years of grandeur never gave?
And if his eyes shall sleep to wake no more,
   Thy smile will vanish in his troubless grave.

THE RIVIERA, 1894.

CALM Nature, in thy blue Italian guise,
   How vainly dost thou smile upon a mind
   Which, seeing beauty, is to beauty blind.
Yet smile thou on.   Thou canst not sympathise
With any wearied thing that droops or dies.
   And so, adieu.   With   strength   and   hope
      resigned,
   'Tis well that I should soon and surely find
The peace of unawakenable eyes.

That smile will then be no less warm and bright
   For all thy children still untired of play
And strong in growing powers of young delight ;
   Yet, O my dearest, come at times with
      flowers
   In darling memory of those short hours
We shared together as a holiday.

HEBREWS II. 10

(Easter Day, 1894.)

AMEN, now lettest Thou Thy servant, Lord,
Depart in peace, according to Thy Word.
Although mine eyes may not have fully seen
Thy great salvation, surely there have been
Enough of sorrow and enough of sight
To show the way from darkness into light ;
And Thou hast brought me, through a wilderness
  of pain,
To love the sorest paths, if soonest they attain.

Enough of sorrow for the heart to cry,
' Not for myself, nor for my kind, am I ;'
Enough of sight for Reason to disclose,
' The more I learn the less my knowledge
  grows.'   .
Ah, not as citizens of this our sphere,
But aliens militant we sojourn here,
Invested by the hosts of Evil and of Wrong
Till Thou shalt come again with all Thine Angel
  throng.

G

As Thou hast found me ready to Thy call,
Which ordered me to watch the outer wall,
And, quitting joys and hopes that once were
    mine,
To pace with patient step this narrow line,
Oh, may it be that, coming soon or late,
Thou still shalt find Thy soldier at the gate,
Who then may follow Thee till sight needs not to
    prove,
And faith shall be dissolved in knowledge of
    Thy love.

A TALE OF THE SEA

G 2

NOTE

The poem which follows, written some time between 1886 and 1889, appeared in 'Longman's Magazine' for May 1895. In a note appended to it the writer stated that it was 'an historically accurate narration of fact.'

A TALE OF THE SEA

You want a yarn ? Then listen to a story of the
    sea,
About as prime, I take it, as a story well could be,
And one which I can tell first-hand, because I
    saw it all ;
Besides which 'tis so wondrous good all round
    there ain't no call
For me to pull the bow a bit ; so here's my hand
    to you
That, as I hope for my salvation, all I say is true.
We hailed from Liverpool, in autumn time, bound
    for New York ;
Our craft a sailing vessel, good to float as any
    cork.
We were well found in everything, specially in
    the crew,
Which were as fine a lot of fellows as I ever knew.

When we were out a week the wind was blowing
    sou'-sou-'west,
And every swell we rode upon showed us a
    broader chest :
Next day we met the gale, and all next night it
    grew,
And all the day and night that followed harder
    still it blew,
Until it was the biggest storm that I have ever
    seen,
Though I have sailed on every sea since I was
    young and green.
And all on board agreed it was the biggest they
    had known :
Bedad, sir, you might fancy that the ocean had
    been blown
Into the sky ; for winds and waves, and clouds
    and spray, and dark and light
Were all mixed up together, like a mob in a
    furious fight.
We set our course north-west by north, took in all
    sails but three,
And wondered how the ship could live in such a
    maniac sea :

But nobly and right well she rose upon each
    mountain wave—
Threw up her head to meet the foe defiantly and
    brave ;
Bowed down her head when he had passed, to
    gather strength again,
And so was always ready for the giants of the
    main.
It was when drawing near to noon that, on our
    starboard bow,
We saw a vessel labouring among those fields of
    snow :
So far as we could then make out she seemed to
    be all right,
But, as the waves were running over thirty feet in
    height,
We only saw in glimpses that a ship was there
    at all ;
And, Lord, the air was full of mist as at your
    Horse-Shoe Fall.
But by-and-by we spied her flag—the stars and
    stripes quite plain,
And, God Almighty! they were hung reversed
    upon the main!

So down we bore upon her course, and, in an
  hour or two,

Were near enough to see her well, and even count
  her crew.

Now, Bill, the mate, was bold, and strong as any
  two or three,

A tawny British lion—Lord, a very devil he,

Who laughed before the face of Death, shook
  Danger by the hand,

And why the world should shun his friends could
  never understand.

'So here's a go, my men,' he cried : 'a Yankee in
  distress !

Who cares to take a pleasure trip in go-to-meeting
  dress ?'

A dozen hands went up at once, and they prepared
  a boat

Before they told the captain that their notion was
  afloat ;

But, when he heard it, up he rounded on to Bill,
  and said,

'The devil take you for a lunatic, both born and
  bred !

Do you suppose a boat could live in such a sea as
    that,

Or you come out of it if you had th' nine lives of
    a cat?

You are a crazy Scotchman, sir, and if you want
    to drown

Jump overboard, and let us see if that will cool
    your crown.'

So 'gin the boat the men stood still, and looked
    upon the sea :

Indeed, the captain had spoke the truth, as true as
    true could be :

But all the answer Bill had made was, 'You are
    skipper here,

And maybe Scotch to English are as whiskey is
    to beer.'

'Twas then I looked to see how yet the Yankee
    craft might fare,

When, by my faith, the stars and stripes no longer
    floated there :

So out I sang, 'The flag has gone! By Jove, it's
    blown away!'

And every eye was turned to look to where the
    Yankee lay :

But not a single star or stripe from stem to stern
    was shown,
Though no one dreamed the wonderment that
    shortly would be known,
For even while we looked the stars and stripes
    appeared again,
Right briskly running up the mizzen rigging to
    the main ;
But now, although we scarcely could believe our
    very eyes,
The colours floated right side up! Here, then,
    was a surprise ;
The Yankee meant to signal that her danger was
    all past ;
She swam as right as we were, said her colours
    from the mast.
Thereon we raised a bit of cheer, for right well
    glad were we
That no one now could feel a call to face that
    frightful sea.
So calmly for a time we watched her, plunging in
    and out
Among the waves, and not a man among us had
    a doubt

But some mishap had fallen, and been set to rights
    again,
Just at the time when we had got our boat's gear
    into train.
' Go, fetch my glass,' the captain cried ; ' it's rum
    behaviour this,
To call us up by flag reversed, and then to blow
    a kiss.'
Agin the mast, with glass as firm as limpet on a
    rock,
Between the heavings of the sea he watched the
    shuddering shock,
As wave by wave leaped on her deck, like wolves
    with shining teeth,
And hung their claws upon her sides to drag her
    underneath,
Though still she rose and shook them off, as one
    by one they came,
A hungry and an endless pack on hunt of wounded
    game ;
Above the tempest we could hear them roaring
    round their prey,
And saw her plunge among them like a mighty
    beast at bay.

And while we watched her agony it seemed a
    desperate case,

With all her body broken, and with death upon
    her face ;

But still the stars and stripes were flying bravely
    over all,

So still we thought that they had never meant our
    help to call,

But only signalled that we should stand by to
    watch and wait,

For sailors best know how to steer 'twixt Too-
    soon and Too-late.

But Bill, whose sight was wondrous good, was
    staring like a ghost,

And muttered, ' Damn my eyes if e'er she sees
    the coast.'

With that I turned to watch the captain standing
    'gin the mast,

And, as I turned, he dropped the glass all sudden :
    ' Sinking fast ! '

He said no more just then : perhaps it was the
    driving spray,

But I believe I saw him brush a woman's tear
    away.

Yet soon we heard his voice again, as strong as
    strong could be :
'Now, boys, you know the meaning of a Yankee-
    doodle spree ;
He makes his colours turn a somersault before
    they go beneath,
For sure as you are standing there he's face to face
    with death ;
But he would show the Britisher he's not afraid
    to die,
When all his hope of life is that the Britisher
    should try
A desperate rescue through that demoniac sea—
    Hush, boys !'—
For we began a round hurrah—'no time for
    empty noise :
I tell you that I don't believe a rescue can be
    done :
In all my life I never saw a sea so ugly run,
And if you know me, boys, you know that sooner
    than play white
I'd throw my tongue upon the deck to show I'd
    spoken right ;

But I am skipper here, and duty bids me tell you
    plain,
Whoever leaves this ship to-day will not return
    again.
You volunteers are made of right good British
    stuff, I know ;
And this the Yankee knows, yet sees a rescue is
    no go.
Believe me, lads, the Yankee's right ; and brave
    as right is he :
Hats off before the glory of the heroes of the
    sea.'
And then we stood in silence, with our hats held
    in our hands,
As men who need not speak again, where each
    man understands ;
And understands a sight so great that words are
    useless things,
And speech is frozen at its source, while thought
    is taking wings.
Then came a fearful wave astern, much taller than
    the rest,
A moving, toppling mountain with the snow upon
    its crest,

And high above the stars and stripes we saw it
   rear and fall :

Oh, God! she had been sunk before our eyes—
   hull, masts, and all—

A whole ship swallowed by one wave, which
   passed along again,

With but a streak of foam to show the place where
   she had lain.

Without a breath we looked upon that tombstone
   of the deep,

And not a heart but felt a heave as in a nightmare
   sleep ;

But not for long before the waking all on sudden
   came,

For 'mid the white a black rose up—a ship, but
   not the same.

The stars and stripes were gone, with masts, and
   yards, and sails ; the deck

And hull were all that could be seen : the Yankee
   was a wreck.

Yet to the stumps the crew were lashed, and we
   could count them all,

Though every wave now buried them and rolled
   her like a ball.

Then roundly sang out Bill, ' By God, sir, I can't
    stand to see
These men go down before my eyes; 'tis like
    enough, if we
Attempt a rescue, we shall follow in their wake;
    but hark,
My men, if I shall live a hundred years that
    Yankee bark
Will haunt me day and night, like any phantom
    ship where Death
Is grinning in the shrouds; and what's the use o'
    drawing breath
If ever and again it is to think I might ha'
    gi'en
Those Yankee lads a chance? 'Twere all like
    murder to ha' been
So near and watch 'em drown, wi'hout a hand or
    foot to stir:
I'd rather death than buy my life wi' such a
    thought. Aye, sir,
You're right to tell us 'tis foolhardy; that we
    know it is;'
But, lads, I canna' bide to see the Yankee go like
    this.

If he had left his colours topsy-turvy on the
    mast,
Maybe I might ha' held my peace, and watched
    him to the last ;
But, Lord, I canna' stand you running right side
    up, my friend,
And now I'd rather go wi' you than stay to see
    the end.'
A shout went up, as with one voice, to tell the
    captain there
That all his crew were British tars, who lived to
    do and dare ;
For Bill had said what all had felt, and we were
    by his side,
To make the captain give the word, whatever
    might betide.
No time for parley then, and so he quickly
    answered, ' Aye—
Now sharp, brave lads, be off, be off, to rescue
    or to die !
All hands to starboard, lads ; let go the boat, with
    Bill to steer.'
Eight volunteers, and Bill as cox, jumped in above
    the gear ;

But, gad, sir, never in our lives was such a job
    as that,
For all the while our ship was tumbling like an
    acrobat,
And half the time we heeled to beam ends on our
    starboard side,
Then back again to beam ends on our larboard,
    while we tried
To catch the level moment, as we rolled betwixt
    the two,
For dropping with a sudden rush the lifeboat and
    her crew.
Hung on the stays, with all their oars spread
    waiting in the air,
They looked more like a thing to fly than such a
    sea to dare,
And in each face of all the nine there was a pair
    of eyes
That showed the very devil of a man who does or
    dies,
While up into the sky, and down again into the
    sea,
We all were holding anxiously, as silent as could
    be.

Then suddenly sung out the word, ' Let go,' and
    down they went!

Good God! a moment afterwards, with all our
    bodies bent

Athwart the gunwale, not a sign or vestige could
    we find,

So turned our eyes with horror to the waste of
    waves behind.

There, battling in the tempest, nine strong swim-
    mers might we see,

Without a hope of helping them in their last
    agony,

When, by the Mass, as down we dipped to star-
    board side again,

We saw her high above our heads, and cheered
    with might and main ;

For all the eight were pulling for their very lives
    away,

Mixed up in mountain waves of foam and strug-
    gling in the spray.

So they drew on, and on and on, and on and on
    they drew,

But only now and then it was they glimpsed into
    our view,

H 2

And ever and anon we thought—they were so
    long unseen—
They never more would show above the crests
    that rolled between.
Ah, sir, it is a dreadful sight to watch a boat that
    braves
A thousand odds to reach a wreck among a thou-
    sand waves ;
And never since the world began is any sight
    more grand
Than when at last the rope is thrown which joins
    them hand in hand.
Next one by one we saw the shipwrecked men
    pass down the line,
Now high in air, then plunging down in fathoms
    deep of brine,
Till all were got aboard and stowed to balance up
    the boat,
Which rode so deep it seemed to us she could no
    longer float ;
But Bill was at the tiller, and no man could steer
    like Bill,
So on they came, while cheer on cheer we raised
    with right good will,

Until at last the rope was thrown which joined us
    hand in hand,
And every man was hauled on deck, as safe as on
    the land.
Next day the storm had lulled, and when, with
    blankets and with rum,
We got some show of life in the new faces that
    had come,
Our skipper says to theirs, ' Now tell us all your
    yarn, my man.'
With that the Yankee spat a spit, squared up, and
    thus began :—
' My tale's soon told,' quoth he : ' 'twas yesterday
    we sprang a leak,
And as the gale grew stronger, sir, our vessel
    grew more weak.
She strained, and writhed, and groaned, just like
    a living thing in pain,
And all night long we worked the pumps, but
    worked them all in vain ;
For hour by hour the water gained through all the
    dismal night,
And when the morning broke at last the gale was
    at its height.

You bet we were exhausted as a flock of prairie
    hens
When blown to sea and fluttering with no more
    strength than wrens :
The cargo was all overboard, and yet we rode so
    low
I saw the pumps were useless, and prepared the
    boats to go ;
But early in the morning they were stove and
    washed away,
So then we lashed each other fast, and waited for
    the day.
Right glad were we to see your sail bear down on
    us at noon,
And ran our colours wrong side up, for you were
    none too soon.
"A Union Jack! a Union Jack!" we cried;
    " Oh, blessed sight !
No chicken-hearted lubbers there, but sea-hawks
    born to fight.
Old England to the rescue! Mother England,
    bless thy face!
Brave Britisher, press onward—onward—neck
    and neck thy race

With Death astride the hurricane, in frantic,
    foaming speed."
The hungry distance lessened, and we knew you
    saw our need :
For then we saw you round your boat, like ants
    about a fly,
And knew you meant a rescue—or leastways to
    have a try.
But then it was that first we marked the heights
    that rolled between,
For when your masts went under devil one of
    them was seen ;
And all the sea was like a churn : Lord, how the
    breakers hissed,
And swirled, and raced, and splashed, as if to show
    how they could twist
A boat to matchwood. Then our voices ceased,
    for every heart
Was filling with one thought : each knew it well,
    but whose the part
To speak it out ? Not mine, the skipper of a
    drowning crew,
Leastways not till the others saw what I already
    knew.

Ah, bitter, and yet sweet, it was to see them
whisper then,

For sure was I that what they spoke was spoken
up like men :

I saw it in each darkened face, in each determined
eye :

It was a council to agree that all on board should
die.

At last the mate, as spokesman, came before the
mast, and said,

" We guess the thing's impossible.   The men's as
good as dead

Who should attempt to cross that sea.   Now,
skipper, what say you ?

My mates and me have had a talk, and talked the
business through.

We have no stomach for the sight these Britishers
prepare :

You know as well as we do what it is that waits
them there :

And can you think, when our turn comes, that
Death will seem less grim

Because we saw the Britishers walk into Hell with
him ?

Nay, skipper, we would rather die as honest men
    and true,

Without that awful spectacle first spread before
    our view,

To haunt our dying memories with every dying
    face

That then will look upon us like a witness of dis-
    grace ;

For now we may prevent in time the launching of
    their boat

By running up our Yankee flag as it should always
    float.

Tell, skipper, are you with us, or will you that
    they shall try ?

You see it is impossible : wish you to watch them
    die ? "

With that I spoke up what I thought ; but added
    at the last

That wives and babes should join in council held
    before the mast.

" Ah, skipper," said the mate, " you know that
    there you hit me hard ;

And, gad, you nearly win the game by playing
    such a card :

But I have thought of her and them through all
    the night and day,
Expecting, hoping, waiting for the father far
    away,
Who never, never, never shall come back to see
    them more.
My widow, oh, my orphans, would that you had
    gone before!"
Then stood he straight upright again, and gave a
    gulp or two,
For he had doubled up along with grief for them.
    " But you,"
He cried—" the time is short.   Oh, mates, give
    heed and think again :
These splendid fellows will come on, and will come
    on in vain ;
Their English hearts will perish in the broad
    Atlantic wave,
And English hearts will mourn them as the true
    that mourn the brave ;
For English wives, and English children, wait for
    them at home ;
Ah, would you haunt those homes, like ours, with
    feet that never come ? "

Then, fearing waste of time, I called a vote of
    hands to show,
When, as I live, all went for Aye, and never one
    for No !
Confound me, sir, if I had thought a vote like
    that to find—
A whole ship's crew, and not a man who was not
    of one mind.
So out I sang, " Down with the flag, and up again
    as fast ;
The Britishers will watch us sink, and understand
    at last :
Then all the world shall hear the tale the Britishers
    shall tell,
And proudly every heart in broad America shall
    swell."
So, when the flag was righted, and we saw the
    monstrous wave,
We drew our breath and waited for the water and
    the grave ;
Yet when it broke upon us, with its towering tons
    of weight,
My only thought in death and darkness was,
    " God, Thou art great."

The rest you know in part, though you can never
    rightly know
The adoration you inspired in that terrific row.
And when upon your English deck I clasped your
    English hands
It seemed to draw the union close between our
    native lands ;
For thus in mid Atlantic met, as kindred tried and
    true,
I felt that not unworthy we of brothers such as
    you.'

PRINTED BY
SPOTTISWOODE AND CO., NEW-STREET SQUARE
LONDON

www.ingramcontent.com/pod-product-compliance
Lightning Source LLC
Chambersburg PA
CBHW030620270326
41927CB00007B/1254